OUR SENSES

How Hearing Works

Sally Morgan

PowerKiDS
press.

New York

Published in 2011 by The Rosen Publishing Group Inc.
29 East 21st Street, New York, NY 10010

First Edition

Editor: Nicola Edwards
Designer: Robert Walster
Picture researcher: Shelley Noronha
Series consultant: Kate Ruttle
Design concept: Paul Cherrill

Library of Congress Cataloging-in-Publication Data

Morgan, Sally.
   How hearing works / Sally Morgan. — 1st ed.
      p. cm. — (Our senses)
   Includes index.
   ISBN 978-1-61532-552-8 (library binding)
   ISBN 978-1-61532-557-3 (paperback)
   ISBN 978-1-61532-558-0 (6-pack)
   1. Hearing—Juvenile literature. I. Title.
   QP462.2.M67 2011
   612.8'5—dc22
   5703   2009044492

Photographs:
Cover, 18 istockphoto; title page © Joson/zefa/Corbis;
2, 15 James Steidl/istockphoto; 4 Mark Evans/
istockphoto; 5 Rich Legg/istock; 6 © Will & Deni
McIntyre/Corbis; 7 © Ned Frisk/Corbis; 9, 10, 12,
20, 23 Martyn f. Chillmaid; 11 Ecoscene/Karl Ammann;
13 Ecoscene/Dennis Johnson; 14 Paul Avis/Getty
Images; 16 © epa/Corbis; 17 Ecoscene/Alan Towse;
19 Ecoscene/Brian Cushing; 21 © Richard T. Nowitz/
Corbis; 22 (tl) Ecoscene/Michael Maconachie; (tr) 22
039081 Ecoscene/Fritz Polking; (bl) Daniel Cardiff/
istockphoto; (br) Galina Barskaya/istockphoto

Manufactured in China
CPSIA Compliance Information: Batch #WAS0102PK: For Further Information
contact Rosen Publishing, New York, New York at 1-800-237-9932

Web Sites

Due to the changing nature of Internet
links, PowerKids Press has developed
an online list of Web sites related to
the subject of this book. This site is
updated regularly. Please use this link
to access this list:
http://www.powerkidslinks.com/os/hear

Contents

Hearing

Our world is full of sound. We hear people talking, birds singing, and phones ringing. There are noisy sounds, too. Shouting and slamming doors make loud sounds.

A race car's engine makes a loud noise.

Hearing is one of our five senses.
We hear sounds with our ears.

We use our ears when we listen to somebody talking.

Our five senses
are hearing, sight,
taste, touch,
and smell.

Everyday Sounds

We use different words to describe sounds. Sounds can be loud or soft. They can bang, pop, ring, or rattle.

Can you think of words to describe all the sounds you would hear in this busy street?

We enjoy listening to some sounds, such as musical sounds. Noise is a jumble of loud, harsh sounds that are not pleasant to hear.

People enjoy making and listening to music.

Each musical instrument makes a different sound.

Our Ears

We have two ears. There is one ear on each side of your head. Look at the shape of your ear in a mirror.

The ear's funnel shape makes it good at collecting sounds.

When the ear hears a sound,
a message passes to the brain.
The brain identifies the sound.

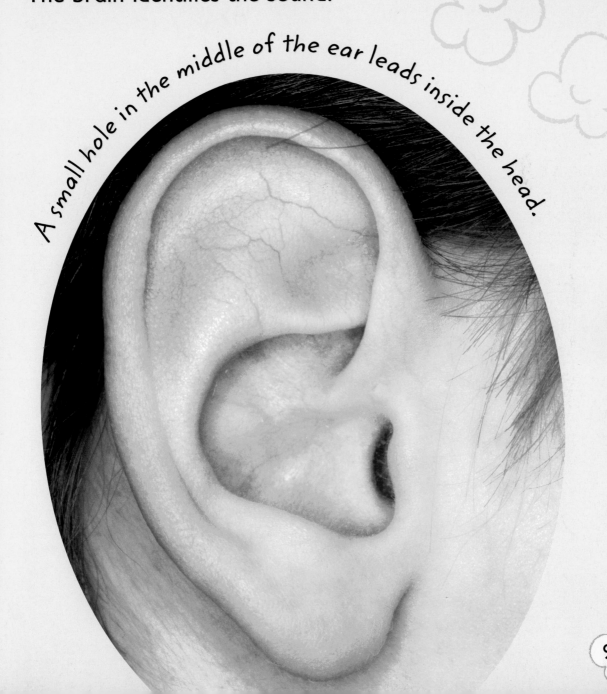

A small hole in the middle of the ear leads inside the head.

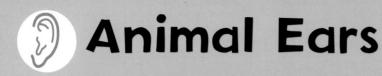

Animal Ears

Ears come in different shapes and sizes. Animals with very good hearing usually have large ears.

Rabbits have long, upright ears that can hear quiet sounds.

Elephants can hear very well. They have the largest ears of any animal.

Elephants can flap their ears to help them to keep cool.

Which Direction?

If a sound comes from the left, the sound reaches the left ear first. A sound from the right reaches the right ear first.

If you cover one ear, it is more difficult to figure out the direction of a sound.

A sound that comes from in front
or from behind, reaches both ears
at the same time.

Zebras can point their ears forward
to hear sounds more clearly.

Loud sounds

Loud sounds are easy to hear. The rumble of a loud explosion or thunder can be heard from far away.

In stormy weather we see lightning and then we hear thunder.

The sirens of police cars and fire engines make loud sounds. When people hear the siren, they move out of the way.

The siren of a fire engine sounds louder as it gets nearer and gets quieter as it moves away.

 # Danger!

Sounds can be dangerous. If we listen
to loud sounds for a long time,
we can damage our hearing.

Some musicians wear earplugs to protect their hearing.

People working in noisy places,
such as airports and building sites,
have to protect their ears.

This worker
is wearing
ear muffs
to protect
his ears
from the
noise of
the drill.

17

Quiet Sounds

Some sounds are quiet. Rain falling into puddles, cats padding across the floor, and leaves rustling in the wind are quiet sounds.

Whispering is talking very softly, so nobody else can hear.

Large ears trap more sounds. If you cup your hand around your ear, the funnel shape makes sounds louder and easier to hear.

With their large ears, bat-eared foxes can hear insects moving about at night.

Some animals have extra-large ears so they can hear quiet sounds.

Hearing Problems

Some people with hearing problems wear a hearing aid. A hearing aid picks up sounds and makes them louder.

A hearing aid helps this girl to hear what her teacher is saying.

Some people cannot hear at all.
They use their fingers to talk to
other people in sign language.

These children are learning how to use sign language.

Glossary and Further Information

brain the control center of the body, found inside the head

ear guards coverings for the ears that protect them from loud noise

earplugs small pieces of plastic worn inside the ears to protect them from loud sounds

funnel a cone-shaped device that is wide at one end and narrow at the other

hearing aid a device that people can wear in their ears to help them hear better

senses functions of the body through which we gather information about our surroundings

sign language a way of talking to someone by using hand shapes

Books

Animals And Their Senses: Animal Hearing
by Kirsten Hall
(Weekly Reader Early Learning Library, 2005)

The Sense of Hearing
by Elaine Landau
(Children's Press, 2009)

World of Wonder: Hearing
by Nick Winnick
(Weigl Publishers, 2009)

You Can't Taste Pickle With Your Ear
by Harriet Ziefert
(Blue Apple Books, 2006)

Index